2/16

GREAT HORNED OWLS

by Melissa Hill

Consulting Editor:
Gail Saunders-Smith, PhD

Content Consultant:
Jessica Ehrgott
Bird and Mammal Trainer,
Downtown Aquarium, Denver

CAPSTONE PRESS
a capstone imprint

Pebble Plus is published by Capstone Press,
1710 Roe Crest Drive, North Mankato, Minnesota 56003
www.capstonepub.com

Library of Congress Cataloging-in-Publication Data
Hill, Melissa, 1975– author.
Great Horned Owls/by Melissa Hill.
pages cm.—(Pebble Plus. Owls)
Summary: "Simple text and full-color photographs describe great
horned owls"—Provided by publisher.
Audience: Ages 5–8.
Audience: K to grade 3.
Includes bibliographical references and index.
ISBN 978-1-4914-6047-4 (library binding)
ISBN 978-1-4914-6053-5 (paperback)
ISBN 978-1-4914-6067-2 (eBook pdf)
1. Great horned owl—Juvenile literature. I. Title.
QL696.S83H54 2015
598.9'7—dc23   2015005326

Editorial Credits
Jeni Wittrock, editor; Juliette Peters, designer; Morgan Walters, media researcher;
Katy LaVigne, production specialist

Photo Credits
Alamy: William Leaman, (owl) bottom left 3; Getty Images: Daniel J Cox, 15, Nick Ridley, 13,
Tom Vezo, 9; iStockphoto: BirdImages, 11, iculizard, 5, JillLang, 22; Minden Pictures: Donald
M. Jones, 17; National Geographic Creative: ROBBIE GEORGE, 19; Shutterstock: Artography,
(mossy bark texture) cover and throughout, (red bark texture) background 3, DnDavis, (owl
image) cover, Eric Isselee, (parakeet) bottom right 6, Eric Isselee, (owl) back cover, bottom left
6, J. Helgason, (tree stump) back cover, 2, 24, jadimages, (clouds treeline) back cover, 1, 2, 23, 24,
Lisa Hagan, 21, Matt Cuda, 7, Scenic Shutterbug, inset 1, Stawek, (map) 8

Note to Parents and Teachers

The Owls set supports national curriculum standards for science related to
life science. This book describes and illustrates great horned owls. The images
support early readers in understanding the text. The repetition of words and
phrases helps early readers learn new words. This book also introduces early
readers to subject-specific vocabulary words, which are defined in the Glossary
section. Early readers may need assistance to read some words and to use the
Table of Contents, Glossary, Read More, Internet Sites, Critical Thinking Using
the Common Core, and Index sections of the book.

Printed in China by Nordica
0415/CA21500542
042015   008837NORDF15

Table of Contents

Owl at Home

Hoo-hoo-hoo! Hooo hoo!

An owl calls out from a tree.

The pointy feathers on his head look like horns.

He's a great horned owl.

Great horned owls are
some of the biggest owls in
North and South America.
Their wingspan can be up
to 5 feet (1.5 meters) long.

Size Comparison

great horned owl
length:
18–25 inches
(46–63 centimeters)

parakeet
length:
6–8 inches
(15–20 centimeters)

Great horned owls live in North and South America. They are found in deserts, forests, and backyards.

Great Horned Owl Range Map

North America

Europe

Asia

Africa

South America

Australia

where great horned owls live

Hidden Hunter

Great horned owls hunt at night. Their feathers match the tree bark. Hidden in trees, great horns watch and listen for prey.

A great horn hears a mouse below. The owl swoops toward the sound. With its strong feet, the owl grabs the mouse. **Dinnertime!**

Great horned owls hunt many
animals. Mice, rabbits, snakes,
and birds are their prey.
They will even eat skunks!

Great-Horned Families

In spring, female great horns lay one to four eggs. They use nests made by other birds. In a month fluffy chicks hatch.

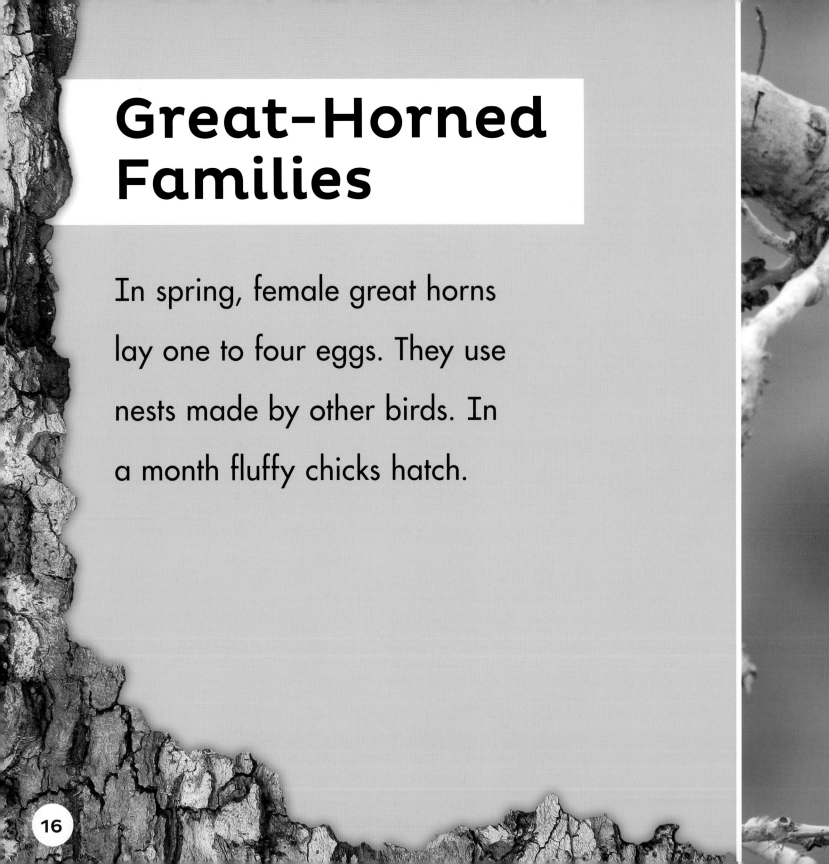

One or both parents bring back food to the nest. Young owls grow quickly. In three months they are able to fly.

A **Long Life**

Great horned owls have very few predators. People are their biggest danger. Great horns live up to 18 years in the wild.

GLOSSARY

chick—a young owl

danger—something that is not safe

desert—an area of land that gets very little rain

hatch—to break out of an egg

predator—an animal that hunts other animals for food

prey—an animal that is hunted by another animal for food

swoop—to fly down quickly

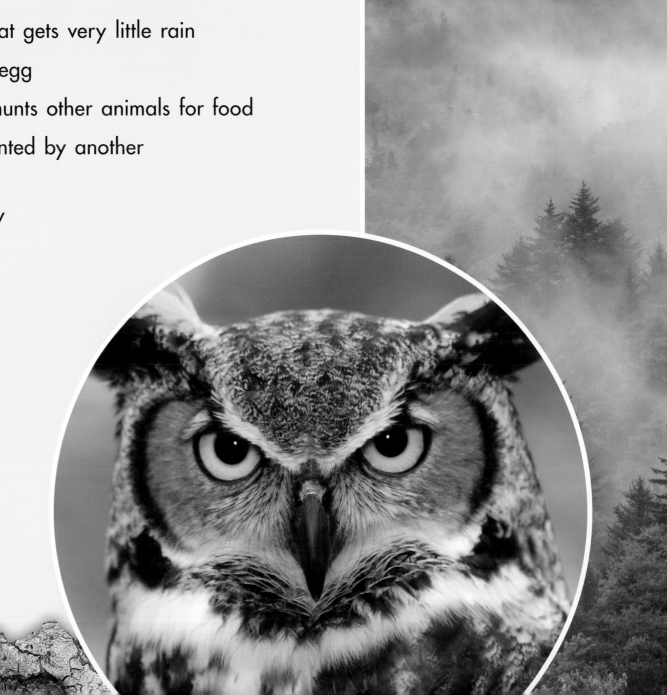

READ MORE

Dunn, Mary. *Owls.* Nocturnal Animals. North Mankato, Minn.: Capstone Press, 2012.

Leaf, Christina. *Great Horned Owls.* North American Animals. Minneapolis: Bellwether Media, 2015.

Spilsbury, Richard. *Invasive Species in the Air.* Invaders from Earth. New York: PowerKids Press, 2015

INTERNET SITES

FactHound offers a safe, fun way to find Internet sites related to this book. All of the sites on FactHound have been researched by our staff.

Here's all you do:

Visit *www.facthound.com*

Type in this code: 9781491460474

Check out projects, games and lots more at
www.capstonekids.com

CRITICAL THINKING USING THE COMMON CORE

1. What makes great horned owls appear to have horns? (Key Ideas and Details)

2. Humans are the biggest threat to great horned owls. What do humans do that might be dangerous to great horns? (Integration of Knowledge and Ideas)

INDEX

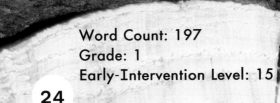

Word Count: 197
Grade: 1
Early-Intervention Level: 15